The Dange

MW01469217

~~Copyright~~
Hilltop Publications
Timothy S. Luchon
Pastor of Hilltop Baptist Church Hunker, Pennsylvania
B.T, Th.M.

This book is copyrighted only to preserve the author's right to his own work. Any part of this work may be used without the author's permission. All that is asked is that proper credit be given, and that no other Bible other than the King James be used in conjunction with this work.

The only Scripture quotations used, copied and believed to be true in the English language, are taken from the 1611 Authorized Version (King James)

Printed by Hilltop Publications United States of America

First Printing – 2013

Hilltop Publications
280 Stone Church Road
Hunker, PA 15639
Phone (724) 925-7100

Table of Contents

INTRODUCTION

In John chapter 8, the Lord Jesus is seen dealing with a group of people who assumed many things about Him. It hit me that these were in conversation with a person of absolutely perfect thoughts and sinless in His life and character.

That got my attention as to the fact that if those people assumed things about and concerning the God-Man, how much more are we as sinful human beings, susceptible to people assuming things about us? Moreover, how much do we assume without thought that our brain may be also guilty of assuming things!

This is not an easy subject to write about. I have taught some of these things at our church and at first I found very strong opposition to these truths.

That told me that I was on to something that absolutely needed to be taught, preached, and applied.

In teaching and preaching these lessons, I began to see people helped by them. So I decided to put some of the basics together in more of an outline form than that of a book.

In preparation and in the teaching of these principles, I learned much about other people who were guilty of assuming; but I must say that this has helped me to avoid my own assumptions more.

Just the fact of being aware of the dangers of assumptions will cause any relationships to heal, grow, and prosper in the things and work of God.

We are all in need of some lessons on how to gain victory over an assuming mindset.

If we do not think this is so, perhaps we are the best candidate for these thoughts.

ASSUMPTION:
THE DESTROYER OF ALL RELATIONSHIPS

"He that answereth a matter before he heareth it, it is folly and shame unto him." Proverbs 18:13

One who assumes lives in a world characterized by mental torment. Not only does he who assumes suffer; but also those who are afflicted by the assumptions of such a person. When assumptions are used as the basis for any decision, conclusion, or judgment, there is no way to determine if a right choice was made. This only creates a world of turmoil, trouble, and tumult. The relationships in such a world will always be characterized by confusion, commotion, contention, and chaos.

If assumptions become the main catalyst for a person's decisions, eventually, that individual will not be able to receive counsel from the very Word of God. Their preconceived assumptions will begin to rule out the truth all together. When this occurs, they will judge all things through a mind and heart tainted by skepticism, cynicism, disbelief, uncertainty, doubt, pessimism, suspicion, sarcasm, disparagement, and scorn. None of those words are conducive to a relationship founded upon honesty, trust, truth, and most of all, faith!

If one main reason could be sighted for all strained or failed relationships, I believe that assumptions are at the top of the list.

To assume is to sum up a situation before you have enough facts to support what you think about that person, place or thing.

To gain victory over this an individual must be brought face to face with this truth and simply ask themselves a few searching questions.

1. Could this be why I cannot seem to get along with people in a decent manner?
2. Is this why I am constantly thinking that someone is lying to me, when I have no actual proof that they are doing so?
3. Does this truth reveal why I think people do not understand me?
4. What if this is the reason for my mistrust of people who are willing to help me?

If each person would do a thorough self-evaluation of their own thinking on this matter, I believe that they will discover how detrimental this mindset has been in many of their relationships.

It is God who created words. I believe that words were meant to be understood properly so that there would be no assumption. God wants us to use the choice of our words properly. Words are tools that must be applied to all things. For proper communication to take place, we must understand each other's words, and how each is using those words.

"For my thoughts are not your thoughts, neither are your ways my ways, saith the LORD. For as the heavens are higher than the earth, so are my ways higher than your ways, and my thoughts than your thoughts. For as the rain cometh down, and the snow from heaven, and returneth not thither, but watereth the earth, and maketh it bring forth and bud, that it may give seed to the sower, and bread to the eater: So shall my word be that goeth forth out of my mouth: it shall not return unto me void, but it shall accomplish that which I please, and it shall prosper in the thing whereto I sent it." Isaiah 55:8-11

It is abundantly clear that The LORD never intended His Written Word to be confusing to those who desire to hear it. It is this very fact that modern-day producers of false translations of the Bible do not seem to understand. They assume that God did not intend for a certain word to produce a specific affect, and calculated results in those who hear His Words. That is why they have the wicked audacity to change and supplement words of God's choosing for their own assumptions of what they think the words of the Bible should say. To do such a thing is the lowest degree of evil in assumption! And those who do so, will suffer exactly the words of Revelation 22:18-19.

"For I testify unto every man that heareth the words of the prophecy of this book, If any man shall add unto these things, God shall add unto him the plagues that are written in this book: And if any man shall take away from the words of the book of this prophecy, God shall take away his part out of the book of life, and out of the holy city, and from the things which are written in this book."

It must be considered that when we assume, we are adding to, or taking away from the words someone speaks to us. Many times people have developed a very bad habit of "reading between the lines."

We must discipline ourselves to avoid this tendency. If not, we will never be conversing in reality with man or God!

There are words closely related to the word assumption. These must be understood in order to see the full meaning of assumption.

For instance, the word "presume" is very close to assume, but it is used in a more *positive sense.* Both of these words are used for things conceived in the mind without necessarily having any external basis for such conclusions. These words deal with thoughts, ideas and concepts in the mind.

PRESUME

- To take or suppose to be true or entitled to belief, **without examination** or positive proof, or on the strength of probability. (We presume that a man is honest, who has not been known to cheat or deceive; **but even in this we are sometimes mistaken**.)

This word shows us that it is not wise to *presume*, but to *assume* is worse. A presumption can have underlying truth with it; an assumption is nothing but unfounded and false! A presumption could be true; but with an assumption, we cannot know if it is true.

The word perception is also related to these. But even in a perception, we could be wrong. The only one who could perceive things with 100% accuracy was the Lord Jesus. Even as a man, He could do this without error for His motives and understanding of all things were never based upon an assumption.

PERCEIVE

- The act of perceiving or of receiving impressions by the senses; or that act or process of the mind which makes known an external object. In other words, **the notice which the mind takes of external** objects.

ASSUME

1. To take what is not just; to take with arrogant claims; to arrogate; to seize unjustly; as, to assume haughty airs; to assume unwarrantable powers.
2. To take for granted**, or without proof**; to suppose as a fact; as, to assume a principle in reasoning.
3. To take what is **fictitious**; to pretend to possess.
4. To be arrogant; to claim more than is due.

Note: Even when the definition of this word is used in a positive way, it is still a fact that to assume something is to take something upon you that is not actually yours to take!

5. In law, to take upon one's self an obligation; to undertake or promise; as, A assumed upon himself, and promised to pay.

Human beings assume, God cannot assume; for He can do nothing that "could even <u>possibly</u> be found to be false in any way!!!"

Consider these thoughts concerning assumptions.
1. Assumptions are not based on facts.

*"Howbeit when he, the Spirit of **truth**, is come, he will guide you into **all truth**: for he shall not speak of himself; but whatsoever he shall hear, that shall he speak: and he will shew you things to come."* John 16:13

Ephesians 4:22
*"That ye put off concerning **the former conversation** the old man, which is **corrupt** according to the **deceitful** lusts;*

Ephesians 4:23
*"And be renewed in the **spirit of your mind**;"*

Ephesians *4:24*
"And that ye put on the new man, which after God is created in righteousness and true holiness."

13

Ephesians *4:25*
*"Wherefore putting away **lying, speak every man truth** with his neighbour: for we are members one of another."*

2. Assumptions have only a 50/50 chance of being correct.

James 3:10
"Out of the same mouth proceedeth blessing and cursing. My brethren, these things ought not so to be."

James 3:11
"Doth a fountain send forth at the same place sweet water and bitter?"

James 3:12
"Can the fig tree, my brethren, bear olive berries? either a vine, figs? so can no fountain both yield salt water and fresh."

James 3:13
"Who is a wise man and endued with knowledge among you? let him shew out of a good conversation his works with meekness of wisdom."

James 3:14

"But if ye have bitter envying and strife in your hearts, glory not, and lie not against the truth."

James 3:15
"This wisdom descendeth not from above, but is earthly, sensual, devilish."

James 3:16
"For where envying and strife is, there is confusion and every evil work."

James 3:17
"But the wisdom that is from above is first pure, then peaceable, gentle, and easy to be intreated, full of mercy and good fruits, without partiality, and without hypocrisy."

3. Assumptions always breed mistrust of others.

"And many shall follow their pernicious ways; by reason of whom the way of truth shall be evil spoken of." II Peter 2:2

"For there are many unruly and vain talkers and deceivers, specially they of the circumcision:" Titus 1:10

15

4. **Assumptions cannot be properly weighed in the mind.**

Isaiah 59:13-14

"In transgressing and lying against the LORD, and departing away from our God, speaking oppression and revolt, conceiving and uttering from the heart words of falsehood. And judgment is turned away backward, and justice standeth afar off: for truth is fallen in the street, and equity cannot enter."

5. **Assumptions always cause frustration in the one who assumes, and in the one being subject to an assumption.**

Proverbs 18:7

*"A fool's mouth is his destruction, and his lips are the snare of **his** soul."*

Proverbs 26:22

"The words of a talebearer are as wounds, and they go down into the innermost parts of the belly."

6. **Assumptions cause lack of confidence at all levels of relationship:**

Proverbs 25:19

"Confidence in an unfaithful man in time of trouble is like a broken tooth, and a foot out of joint."

   A. An authority toward a subordinate.
   B. A subordinate to authority.
   C. Husbands and wives.
   D. Children and parents.
   E. Teachers and students
   F. Pastor and congregation

1. Assumptions are presumption.

2. Assumptions are guesses.

3. Assumption is conjecture.

4. Assumptions are imaginary.

5. To assume is only to speculate.

6. Assumptions are based on negatives of the past, unfounded ideas in the present, and forecast only imaginary good or bad in the future.

HOW TO DETECT IF A PERSON MAY BE ASSUMING

*"**Why** do ye not understand my speech? even because ye cannot hear my word."* John 8:43

*"When Jesus came into the coasts of Caesarea Philippi, he asked his disciples, saying, **Whom do men say** that I the Son of man am?"* Matthew 16:13

*"Then said Jesus unto the twelve, **Will ye** also go away?"* John 6:67

*"Jesus saith unto him, **Have I been** so long time with you, and yet hast thou not known me, Philip? he that hath seen me hath seen the Father; and how sayest thou then, Shew us the Father?"* John 14:9

The Lord Jesus was the Master of the **searching question**!

He used questions constantly. He did not ask questions because He did not know the answers; He asked questions to **eliminate the assumptions** in the minds of those He desired to help!

If we are to effectively communicate the Word of God to people, we also must learn to ask the right questions. We must hear what is in the minds of those we are attempting to help before we can be effective in doing so. If this method is not used in our teaching and preaching, most likely we will be speaking to minds that are not on the "same page" as we think they are.

I believe that the person attempting to teach or communicate to another person must take the initiative to see that those to whom they are speaking are not assuming. Getting people to think like we are at the time we speak to them must be mastered if we are to help them with our words.

Just being aware that this could be taking place will cause us to be more effective in our reciprocal conversations. If not, our attempts to communicate even the greatest of truth will be one-sided.

Keep in mind that the things to follow could be indicators of assumptions that apply to us and those to whom we speak. Assuming is not always a one way street. We all must do our best not to assume things.

If we desire to effectively communicate to people, and have them communicate to us, we must make ourselves conscious of some indicators of assumption that may be taking place.

Consider the following possible indicators of assumption. Remember, both the speaker and the listener could be guilty to some degree of all of these.

- If people are always attempting to finish your sentences for you, this may be an indicator that they are assuming something other than what you are trying to say.
- If people to whom you are speaking frequently ask you for clarification, this could also be an indicator of possible assumptions.
- Being misquoted as to the context of what you have stated is an indicator.
- Blank or questioning stares.
- Frustration on the part of the speaker or the listener.
- People try to avoid speaking with you.
- People seem to be listening to your advice, but they do not do what they hear.
- People are not able to follow the instructions that are spoken to them.

We all are guilty of many of these things, but we can get victory over them. We must set hearts and minds to take personal responsibility to make sure, as best as we can, they we are not the ones doing the assuming. We must learn to ask the right questions to those listening to us. This will help to relieve as many assumptions as possible.

WHAT CAN CAUSE A PERSON TO ASSUME?

*"This know also, that in the last days perilous times shall come. For men shall be lovers of their own selves, covetous, boasters, proud, blasphemers, disobedient to parents, unthankful, unholy, Without natural affection, trucebreakers, false accusers, incontinent, fierce, despisers of those that are good, Traitors, **heady, highminded**, lovers of pleasures more than lovers of God..."* II Timothy 3:1-4

HEADY is perhaps one of the closest words we can use to give us a word picture of what is in the mind of one who assumes. Look at the definition of this word.

"Rash; hasty; precipitate; violent; disposed to rush forward in an enterprise without thought or deliberation; hurried on by will or passion; ungovernable. Apt to affect the head, violent; impetuous..."

High-minded is also a word that teaches us about those who assume. These will usually be "Proud and arrogant."

Many who teach and preach the Word of God today have to deal with this type of mindset. I believe that assumptions have caused more problems in good churches and among good people than may have been previously detected. And according to the Bible, these *"...perilous times..."* will not get any easier to handle.

Let's look at several Biblically suggested causes for assumptions among God's people.

1. Not having **a renewed mind**.

*"And be renewed in **the spirit of your mind;"***
Ephesians 4:23

At salvation the process of having a renewed mind begins. If a saved person reads the perfectly preserved Word of God, and studies to understand those words, they will have a new mind.

It may be the case as it is so many times that a person truly is saved, but they feed their minds on perversions of what they think are Bibles; these will never have a right mind concerning the truth of God.

It is the Word of God that gives us the right spirit in our minds that is vital and necessary if we are to hear the truth correctly. False versions of the Bible cause a wrong mindset in many areas concerning old fashioned Christianity. Many doctrines cannot be properly assimilated until the natural mind is renewed in the way it thinks and processes information.

2. Not understanding the truth because of not being able to hear the words of the Bible.

*"Why do ye **not understand** my speech? even because ye cannot hear my word."*   John 8:43

This is akin to the first, but this is exclusively aimed at a person who is unsaved.

In I Corinthians 2:14 we are told. *"But the natural man receiveth not the things of the Spirit of God: for they are foolishness unto him: neither can he know them, because they are spiritually discerned."*

Without salvation a person remains in a natural sinful state of mind, and cannot and will not understand the Word of God.

3. Listening to other people for our basis in truth instead of listening to God.

*"When Jesus came into the coasts of Caesarea Philippi, he asked his disciples, saying, **Whom do men say** that I the Son of man am?"* Matthew 16:13

Everything we hear from people must be checked by the Word of God. If we fail to do this, we could assume falsehood is true, just because "others" say something is true.

4. A bad **attitude**.

*"But he turned, and rebuked them, and said, Ye know not what **manner of spirit** ye are of."* Luke 9:55

These disciples got angry at the way some people treated the Saviour. They let that anger control their speech. Even though we could judge that their motive may have been good in their estimation, it was not the way our Lord wants us to treat those who do not understand.

5. A **bad disposition** at the time a person speaks.

*"A good man out of the good treasure of his heart bringeth forth that which is good; and an evil man out of the evil treasure of his heart bringeth forth that which is evil: for of the **abundance of the heart** his mouth speaketh."* Luke 6:45

Many times assumptions come about when our hearts are not under the proper influences. A "bad day" could be allowed to taint our hearts and in turn, the words we speak to others may carry our disposition with them to the ears and hearts of others.

Someone has said in similar terms that it is alright if people get upset with us because of our "position on truth," but we are responsible to not cause them to be mad at us because of our "disposition."

6. A **superiority** complex.
*"I wrote unto the church: but Diotrephes, who loveth to have the **preeminence** among them, receiveth us not."* III John 1:9

Some people let a position or delegated authority go to their heads in such a way that they feel as if they are really in control, when they are not. This is the cause of many hurtful assumptions.

Only God has *"...the preeminence..."* (Colossians 1:18) And isn't it an amazing thought that not even God *FORCES HIS WILL ON ANYONE!*

7. Some people do not take the responsibility to **speak** in such a way that people are not offended.

*"Wherefore, if I come, I will remember his deeds which he doeth, prating against us with **malicious words**: and not content therewith, neither doth he himself receive the*

brethren, and forbiddeth them that would, and casteth them out of the church. " III John 1:10

Sadly to say, many times this may even be the man in the pulpit or a Sunday school teacher.

James 3:1-2 addresses this very clearly.

"My brethren, be not many masters, knowing that we shall receive the greater condemnation. For in many things we offend all. If any man offend not in word, the same is a perfect man, and able also to bridle the whole body.

8. A mind influenced by **vanity**.

*"This I say therefore, and testify in the Lord, that ye henceforth walk not as other Gentiles walk, in the **vanity of their mind**,* " Ephesians 4:17

A vain person lives in a very small world. That world is limited to the confines of the size of the cavity which houses their physical brain. To a person such as this, everything is subject only to what is conceived in a very small world.

9. A **blind** heart.

*"Having the understanding darkened, being alienated from the life of God through the **ignorance** that is in them, **because of the blindness of their heart**:"* Ephesians 4:18

This type of assumption is the result of a heart that is not able to feel normal emotions.

For instance, compassion is an emotion that can be used to help others, or to understand others. Blindness of the heart can be self-induced by the individual who continually rejects the principles of the Word of God.

Blindness of the heart can also be the result of just not knowing the principles of right and wrong as found in the Bible.

This condition can also be the result of the Word of God being removed from the heart of a person by the influence of the devil.

*"When **any one** heareth the word of the kingdom, and understandeth it not, then cometh the wicked one, and **catcheth away** that which was sown in his heart. This is he which received seed by the way side."* Matthew 13:19

10. Lack of Biblical **Separation**.

*"And be not **conformed to this world**: but be ye transformed by the renewing of your mind, that ye may prove what is that good, and acceptable, and perfect, will of God."* Romans 12:2

If a child of God will not separate themselves from the things of the world, as clearly directed by the Word of God, then that person will not have a mind that is able to be discerning as to what is or is not the will of God.

This un-submissive mind will assume that worldly things are acceptable for believers. They will often times seek to justify their worldly appearance and attitudes seemingly with no conscience that A Holy God would never participate nor condone their behavior.

These are often professing believers who end up in ecumenical, charismatic, new evangelical, or other liberal and apostate types of ministries. These will assume that old fashion Biblical Christianity is no longer for our day and time.

Assumptions caused by this level of rebellion are the source of many a good church being torn apart from within. Those who think according to these types of assuming minds will constantly fight against the truth of old fashioned Bible Christianity.

The assumptions that have built up in their minds never seem to allow them to be on the same page as the pastor who is doing his best to lead a church forward and away from the ever-changing influences of this world.

11. A **reprobate** mind.

*"Examine yourselves, whether ye be in the faith; prove your own selves. Know ye not your own selves, how that Jesus Christ is in you, except ye be **reprobates**?* II Corinthians 13:5

This verse is linked to being *"...in the faith..."* God did not create "many faiths," He ordained *"...one faith..."* (Ephesians 4:5, Jude 3) If a professing believer gets involved with a ministry that is not under the authority of a Biblically sanctioned New Testament Church, they will not think correctly when it comes to doctrine and the practice of that doctrine.

12. A **conscience** unable to feel conviction.

*"Speaking lies in hypocrisy; having their **conscience seared** with a hot iron;"* I Timothy 4:2

A person who reaches this depth of assuming will speak lies to others while knowing that they are hypocrites, but they do not care if those they afflict know this.

These will look you in the eye, tell you they are speaking the truth, while in their own hearts they know they are lying to you.

These are unable to feel that this is wrong to do, and they would not care if they did feel something.

The assumptions from such a mind in this sad condition are extremely hurtful to themselves and others, especially to those who love and care for such a person.

Because of the assumptions in the mind of these, we who are dealing in the truth of the Scriptures often feel powerless to help these people. It seems that no matter what you say in an attempt to help them, they reject or twist everything you say into a confusing mess.

OBSERVATIONS ON DEALING WITH THOSE WHO ASSUME

"Now we exhort you, brethren, warn them that are unruly, comfort the feebleminded, support the weak, be patient toward all men." I Thessalonians 5:14

1. When a person assumes, the person they are sinning against cannot answer according to truth, for they do not know what is in the mind of the one assuming.

2. The mind of someone who assumes is in a constant state of uncertainty.

3. People who assume are angry people.

4. People who assume always think others are angry at them, and usually they are right. But the reason people are easily angry at those who assume, is because they cannot figure out the thoughts, or motives of the one who is living in assumptions.

5. A person who assumes cannot be pleased.

6. Those who are forced to deal with such a person must often "walk on eggshells" around one who assumes. They may not know that the individual has a problem with assumptions, but they do understand that it is better to let that person speak, and just try to give in,   agree, and do what they want.

7. One who lives in assumptions has no sure direction in life. They are constantly jumping from one place to another, because in their mind, no place is what they want it to be.

8. When speaking to one who is assuming, it is almost impossible to keep on one thought- line. They will jump back and forth to different and seemingly unrelated thoughts.

9. When attempting to reason with one who assumes, must constantly correct the words of the assumer in an attempt to keep that person on the thought-line.

10. The one reasoning with an assumer often cannot figure out why that person doesn't understand their words, that to him, are very clear and to the point.

11. If you believe someone is assuming as you are speaking with them, you must somehow get control of the conversation.

   a. Stop and ask them if what you are saying makes sense to them.

   b. Ask if they understand your motive for the conversation.

   c. Say to them, "If you were me, how would you state what I am attempting to say to you?

d. Ask them how they would make what is being said more understandable.

e. Always attempt to make the person who is assuming to know that you what to communicate with them in a peaceful manner.

f. If you cannot reason with a person who is assuming, decide if you can continue to fellowship with that person just as they are, or kindly avoid them and the confrontations that may result.

HOW TO GAIN VICTORY OVER ASSUMPTIONS

*"Behold, thou desirest truth in **the inward parts**: and in the hidden part thou shalt make me to know wisdom."* Psalm 51:6

The first step in winning over any fault or sin is to make sure we are not assuming that we do not or could not have a problem a problem with assuming. An assumption such as this will defeat us before we even acknowledge we have a problem. Stop and think of the tragedy if this occurs. An assumption that we do not have a problem with assuming will be the cause of us not gaining victory over assuming!

1. Understand that **our own minds** could be, and most likely are guilty of assuming.

*"Search me, O God, and know my heart: try me, and know **my <u>thoughts</u>**..."* Psalm 139:23

2. This is a personal battle. It is a fight to regain **control of your mind** in order to think only in truth!

"Casting down imaginations, and every high thing that exalteth itself against the knowledge of God, and

*bringing into captivity **every thought** to the obedience of Christ;"* II Corinthians 10:5

3. You must decide that this is a problem with you and set out to **defeat it** with The Word of God. Learn to be proficient in using Scripture to fight your personal battles.

"So shall my word be that goeth forth out of my mouth: it shall not return unto me void, but it shall accomplish that which I please, and it shall prosper in the thing whereto I sent it." Isaiah 55:11

4. Before you assume anything, stop and quote this next verse. In *doing* what this verse teaches, there is no room left for assumptions.

*"Finally, brethren, whatsoever things are **true**, whatsoever things are **honest**, whatsoever things are **just**, whatsoever things are **pure**, whatsoever things are lovely, whatsoever things are of good report; if there be any virtue, and if there be any praise, <u>think on these</u> **things.**"* Philippians 4:8

5. Practice trusting The Lord to reveal things to you from the Scriptures. This may be by reading, or from the preaching and teaching at church.

*"Let us therefore, as many as be perfect, **be thus minded**: and if in any thing ye be **otherwise minded**, God **shall reveal** even this unto you."* Philippians 3:15

Pray and ask God to allow your mind to be subject to knowledge that you do not yet understand at the present concerning assumptions.

*"**Lie not** one to another, seeing that ye have put off the old man with his deeds; And have put on the new man, which is **renewed in knowledge** after the image of him that created him:"* Colossians 3:9-10

6. Pray for a cleansing of your mind from anything that would hinder you from understanding how to avoid assumptions. And take it upon yourself to do what God requires of you to be rid of assumptions.

*"And be not conformed to this world: but be ye transformed by **the renewing of your mind**, that ye may prove what is that good, and acceptable, and perfect, will of God."* Romans 12:2

7. If you cannot *"**PROVE**"* to your own conscience, that your thoughts on a matter are *"good,"* *"acceptable,"* and *"perfect,"* (mature) and that those

thoughts are in line with the *"will of God"*, refuse to go any further into assumptions.

*"And be not conformed to this world: but be ye transformed by the renewing of your mind, that **ye may prove** what is that good, and acceptable, and perfect, will of God."* Romans 12:2

8. Ask God to use the Bible, teaching, and the preaching at church to change any actions that could cause you to not have victory over assumptions.

*"This I say therefore, and testify in the Lord, that ye henceforth walk not as other Gentiles walk, in the **vanity of their mind**, Having the **understanding darkened**, being alienated from the life of God through the **ignorance** that is in them, because of the blindness of their heart: Who being past feeling have given themselves over unto lasciviousness, to work all uncleanness with greediness. But **ye have not so learned** Christ; If so be that ye have heard him, and have been taught by him, as the truth is in Jesus: That ye put off concerning the former conversation the old man, which is corrupt according to the **deceitful** lusts; And **be renewed in the spirit of your mind**;"* Ephesians 4:17-23

9. Ask The Holy Spirit for His help in leading you to a new attitude about assumptions.

*"And **be renewed in the spirit of your mind;** "* Ephesians 4:17

42

FINAL THOUGHTS ON ASSUMPTIONS

"And the servant of the Lord must not strive; but be gentle unto all men, apt to teach, patient, meekness instructing those that oppose themselves; if God peradventure will give them repentance to the acknowledging of the truth; And that they may recover themselves out of the snare of the devil, who are taken captive by him at his will."   II Timothy 2:24-26

To any person attempting to help someone who is plagued by assumptions, these verses can be very helpful. The context is obviously speaking directly to the preacher.

I have no doubt that may of the problems faced between a pastor and the other people in a church body, are caused by, or directly related to assumptions. Yes, this does apply to all relationships and all people, but consider this application for now.

I wonder how many churches have been hurt by an assumption that was never cleared up. In thinking on this subject, I have gone over my past history with people and have found that both I and others have been guilty of assuming.

As a pastor, I have seen that when I do not diligently attempt to remove as many assumptions or possibilities to assume, that relationships are hurt unnecessarily. If I had only asked a few more patient questions, or tried harder to put myself into the mind-set of another, a precious soul could have been helped.

I understand that this is not always the full fault of the pastor, but let's face it; those of us whom God has called, are called to specifically speak to people as a tool of God! We are to be a mouthpiece for Him for the benefit of His people!

As a pastor, a teacher, a preacher, a missionary, or an evangelist, God's servants must be very aware of the potential problems that can arise because of an assumption, no matter who is guilty of such.

I also know that there have been a few situations that have come up, when certain individuals were so steeped in assumptions that no matter what was said to them, they always seemed to hear those things through a maze of conjecture, supposition, and unfounded speculation which surrounds assumptions. At times when this has occurred, the situation seemed almost impossible to correct.

But most of the time, a simple extra question, a little patience, a dose of humility, and stating the same truth in different ways or from another perspective, has proven to eliminate many an assumption.

I know this above all things as pertaining to this subject; just the fact that we each understand that *we* must not assume, and that we each keep a desire to help *others* not to assume, will most likely solve many problems before they ever become a problem!

About The Author

Pastor Timothy Luchon

Pastor T.S. Luchon has pastored for 20 years. He has been involved with many aspects of the ministry. He pastored The Blue Mountain Bible Baptist Church in Thornbury, Ontario Canada for over 6 years; was given the privilege of serving under Dr. Keith Gomez at Northwest Bible Baptist Church and Providence Baptist College in Elgin Illinois for two years, where he served as Missions Director, Dean of Men, Operations Manager, and taught several Bible classes at the College.

While there, he was called to pastor the Hilltop Baptist Church in Hunker, Pennsylvania, where he and Denise, his faithful wife of 36 years now reside.

His unwavering stand on The King James Bible; its inspired and preserved words; and the inspired and preserved **doctrine** of That Bible; has allowed him to help several Independent, Fundamental, Baptist Preachers and Churches to root out Protestant based **doctrines** and the substandard practices they cause.

In the 14 years of pastoring at Hilltop Baptist, he has now written over 30 doctrinally sound books; designed to promote only *"...**the faith** which was once delivered to the saints. (Jude 3)*

TOOLS FOR THE GREAT COMMISSION
SOULWINNING   SERVICE   SEPARATION

For Online Orders Go To...
www.hilltoppublications.org

Dressing Modestly In Dangerous Times

Biblically addressing the dress standards of saved females, from the eyes of a saved male; and a warning as to the other eyes viewing the immodesty of the women in our Baptist Churches. If Women professing godliness; but not convinced to be Biblically modest in their public appearance, could see this subject from the eyes of a male (which by creation is impossible!); they would obey The WORD of The Highest Male Eyes, and go shopping. 26,528 words.

Unto What Then Were Ye Baptized?

The Baptism of John fulfilled its main purpose when he baptized The Lamb of God. That Baptism of Repentance, and The one New Testament Baptism by immersion, were distinctly different in their purpose; yet in each are taught the same seven basic elements. As John's Baptism was the starting point of The Ministry of The Lord Jesus as The Son of God on Earth; so The Lord's one Baptism is now the beginning; of a child of God's service as a member of one of His Churches. 10,883 words.

The Dangers Of Assumption

Have you ever attempted to help someone who claims to be saved; using the Scriptures; but you just cannot seem to get them on the same page? People who assume think and live in a world that does not exist. While a person is assuming; thoughts, feelings, faith, motives, perceptions and the emotions they produce are not real: for they are not based on truth. 6,152 words.

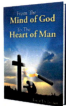

From The Mind Of
God To The Heart
Of Man

Many saved people, including some preachers and self-appointed theologians, do not know how The Written Word of God was transferred to Earth from Its First Edition in Heaven, and how It's Eternally Inspired Words and The Life in each of Them, were eventually copied and Preserved into the pages of The King James Bible. 11,483 words.

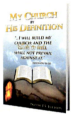

My Church By
His Definition

When The LORD first wrote the word Church is His Book, He had only one kind of Church in mind. Everything surrounding the word Church is so very simple, and the same in each instance of its use through Scripture. This is a simple study tracing the first mention of The word Church from the first writing of the word, up to the final assembly of all who are truly born again. 8,362 words.

Avoiding The
Curse

There are very few things in the lives of Churches, and individual people in general, which affect them more than money. It is sad but true, but nearly everything in this world is in some way influenced or operated by money. Next to pride, money is no doubt the source most responsible for the manipulation of motives toward many things. We who are born again are also susceptible to this "...root of all evil..."

Flesh, Feelings
Or Faith

People who profess to be born again, often continue to live, still subject to some of the same feelings and emotions which dominated their lives before salvation. Those internal leftovers from the past, are not often used for the good of themselves or for others. God's Word teaches clearly, that the feelings and emotions in a saved person, must be under the control of the grace of God.
Feelings and emotions can be wonderful servants; but they are lousy masters.

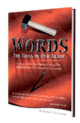

Words The Tools
Of Our Trade

Written Words were The Verbal, Vocal Tools with which The Lord used in the creation of the worlds and all things. It was with those same words by which He Authored our Faith. When other words, which are not found in His Book, are employed in the building of lives and churches; those sub-standard tools will not produce the same kind of structural integrity. 35,171 words.

Seeds From The Hand
Of The Sower

The number one question in our present day is not that of an unsaved person asking "Is there a God?" It is professing believers asking, "Do we have a perfect copy of God's Bible?" This has been the conflict between self-appointed theologians and Bible Believers all the way back to The Garden of Eden. In Genesis 3:1, God recorded Satan's version of that age-old question. The devil began his deception to Eve with the words, "Yea, hath God said...?" Four words caused her, to doubt the authority, the meaning, motive, and consequences of not following the words exactly as God spoke them to her husband.

Forgiveness The Healer
Of All Relationships

Forgiveness: What a wonderful word. Stop, look at it with your eyes; break it down in your mind; and let its power be unlocked and taken into your heart: For-Give-Ness! To bow down before this word will produce an ocean of thought filled with every ingredient of The Salvation a born again person gets to enjoy.
If this word truly lived in the hearts of those who have been forgiven of the penalty of sin; they would reap more of the blessing available to themselves as they use that forgiveness to benefit others.

Don't Muzzle
The Ox

A Biblical plan to help The People in The Lord's Baptist Churches, to be able to receive and benefit from the teaching and preaching of The Ox, whom God placed in the Office of Pastor. 11,582 words.

Dividing The Line
Between Truth & Error

Biblical comparisons between things such as One Pastor or multiple Elders; Division or Rightly Dividing?; The Faith or a Faith?; Spiritual Words or Unholy spirits?; Christians or christianity?; Deacons or Deacon Board?; Leader or Lords? Are you on the right side of The Lines God left to us? 15,517 words.

Things That Are Wanting
In The Constitution Of
His Church

The Church started by The Lord Jesus is 100% definable by The Scriptures. Yet today, even among Independent Baptist Churches; there are differences of Doctrine that should not be allowed to co-exist with The Lord's decrees. The Lord Jesus is The Foundation; and His Doctrine, as once delivered to us, is to be the only structural composition, used in the building of His kind of New Testament Baptist Churches. 34,447 words.

Modesty The
Missing Factor

God created male and female. Many of God's saved females struggle with the subject of where to draw the lines of dressing according to Bible standards. Perhaps if The Holy Spirit would show them just one line over which they must never cross; they could have their hearts settled on this Biblical Doctrine. Here is that one line: God Is A MALE...do not offend His Holy Eyes by appearing immodestly in public; or to dress like HE, as THE MALE would dress. 4,040 words.

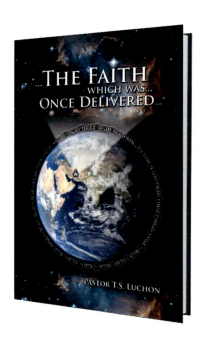

The Faith Which Was
Once Delivered

Many Baptists of the past have learned *"...doctrines..." (Plural)* from the *"...feigned words..."* of what Protestants and others have named Systematic Theology. God's *inspired word,* simply calls what we were supposed to learn; and, for which we have been commanded to *"...contend..;"* .... *"...__the faith__ which was once delivered to the saints." (Jude 3)*

HILLTOP PUBLICATIONS

A MINISTRY OF HILLTOP BAPTIST CHURCH

About Our Ministry:

Hilltop Publications is a ministry under the authority of Hilltop Baptist Church. We are located in Hunker, Pennsylvania about 35 minutes from the city of Pittsburgh. The ministry was founded by Pastor Timothy S. Luchon in 2003 to help churches and ministries be more effective in winning souls. We offer many services such as Book Publishing and Printing, Design & Print Services, Online Bookstore Creation and Website Development.

AFFORDABLE FULL SERVICE BOOK PUBLISHING!

- Book Cover Design
- Inside Book Layout
- Illustration
- Bar Code Generation

- ISBN Registration
- Large Quantity Printing (1000+)
- Small Quantity Printing (50+)
- Laminating & Binding

E-book Creation for :
- *iPhones & iPads*
- *Android Phones & Tablets*
- *PC & Mac*

(724) 925-7100

www.hilltoppublications.org

"...Go out into the highways and hedges, and compel them to come in, that my house may be filled."

Luke 14:23

WEBSITE CREATION & HOSTING

- Website Creation
- Website Hosting
- Domain Name Registration
- Google Search Optimization
- Website Maintenance
- Content Creation
- Website Graphics:
  - *Banners*
  - *Website Logo*
  - *Image Preparation*
  - *Text Layout*

DESIGN & PRINT SERVICES

Logos	Business Cards
Brochures	Custom Tracts
Prayer Cards	Labels
Letterheads	Forms
Envelopes	& Much More!

(724) 925-7100
www.hilltoppublications.org

280 Stone Church Road, Hunker, PA 15639